¡Las mascotas son geniales!
Pets Are Awesome!

MI TORTUGA

MY TURTLE

Norman D. Graubart
Traducción al español: Christina Green

PowerKiDS
press™
New York

Published in 2014 by The Rosen Publishing Group, Inc.
29 East 21st Street, New York, NY 10010

First Edition

Book Design: Colleen Bialecki
Photo Research: Katie Stryker

Traducción al español: Christina Green

Photo Credits: Cover Vitaly Titov & Maria Sidelnikova/Shutterstock.com; p. 5 Carmen Troesser/Aurora/Getty Images; p. 7 Jeff Greenberg/Photo Library/Getty Images; p. 9 Juan Camilo Bernal/Shutterstock.com; p. 11 subin pumsom/Shutterstock.com; p. 13 Darrin Henry/Shutterstock.com; p. 15 Matt Jeppson/Shutterstock.com; p. 17 Danielle Kiemel/Flickr Open/Getty Images; p. 19 Ryan M. Bolton/Shutterstock.com; p. 21 Kenneth M Highfill/Photo Researchers/Getty Images; p. 23 sozaijiten/Datacraft/Getty Images.

Library of Congress Cataloging-in-Publication Data

Graubart, Norman D.
My turtle = Mi tortuga / by Norman D. Graubart ; translated by Christina Green. — First edition.
    pages cm. — (Pets are awesome! = ¡Las mascotas son geniales!)
English and Spanish.
Includes index.
ISBN 978-1-4777-3316-5 (library)
1. Turtles as pets—Juvenile literature. 2. Turtles—Juvenile literature. I. Green, Christina, 1967– translator. II. Graubart, Norman D. My turtle. III. Graubart, Norman D. My turtle. Spanish. IV. Title. V. Title: Mi tortuga.
SF459.T8G7318 2014
639.3'924—dc23
                        2013025093

Web Sites: Due to the changing nature of Internet links, PowerKids Press has developed an online list of websites related to the subject of this book. This site is updated regularly. Please use this link to access the list:
www.powerkidslinks.com/paa/turtle/

Manufactured in the United States of America

CPSIA Compliance Information: Batch # W14PK3: For Further Information contact Rosen Publishing, New York, New York at 1-800-237-9932

CONTENIDO

Las tortugas como mascotas............................ 4

Tipos de tortugas 6

La vida de una tortuga................................. 12

Más sobre las tortugas 18

Palabras que debes saber 24

Índice 24

CONTENTS

Turtles as Pets.. 4

Kinds of Turtles 6

The Life of a Turtle 12

More About Turtles....................................... 18

Words to Know 24

Index 24

Las tortugas son
lindas mascotas.

Turtles are cute pets.

5

Las tortugas pertenecen a la familia de los reptiles. Muchos tipos de tortugas viven en el agua.

Turtles belong to the reptile family. Many kinds of turtles live in water.

7

Las tortugas que viven en la tierra a veces se conocen como tortugas galápago.

Turtles that live on land are sometimes called tortoises.

La **tortuga del desierto** es el reptil del estado de California.

The **desert tortoise** is the state reptile of California.

Algunas tortugas pueden vivir más de 100 años. ¡Esta tortuga tiene casi 180 años!

Some turtles can live for over 100 years. This tortoise is about 180 years old!

Las tortugas ponen **huevos**.

Turtles lay **eggs**.

14

15

Las tortugas bebés se conocen como **crías**.

Baby turtles are called **hatchlings**.

Las tortugas no tienen dientes. Ellas mastican la comida con la quijada.

Turtles have no teeth. They chew food with their jaws.

Esta es una tortuga pintada. Estas tortugas tienen colores brillantes en su caparazón inferior.

This is a western painted turtle. These turtles have bright colors on their bottom shells.

21

Es divertido mirar a las tortugas mascota en sus acuarios.

Pet turtles in their tanks are fun to watch.

PALABRAS QUE DEBES SABER
WORDS TO KNOW

(la) tortuga del desierto
desert tortoise

(los) huevos
eggs

(las) crías
hatchling

ÍNDICE

A
acuario, 22
agua, 6

C
caparazón, 20

D
dientes, 18

G
Galápago, 8

T
tanques, 22
tierra, 8

R
reptil, 6, 10

INDEX

L
land, 8

R
reptile, 6, 10

S
shells, 20

T
tanks, 22
teeth, 18
tortoise(s),
   8, 10

W
water, 6

24